EMMANUEL JOSEPH

The Linguist's Stage, Commanding Multilingual Audiences with Grace and Precision

Contents

1

Chapter 1: The Power of Language

Languages are powerful tools, transcending barriers and connecting people across diverse cultures and backgrounds. As a linguist, mastering multiple languages provides an unparalleled ability to engage with audiences in unique and meaningful ways. The power of language is not just in the words spoken, but in the cultural nuances, gestures, and expressions that accompany them. This chapter will explore the foundational elements of language and the importance of cultural context in effective communication.

The first step in commanding multilingual audiences is understanding the role of language in human interaction. Language shapes our thoughts, influences our behavior, and reflects our identity. For a linguist, recognizing these aspects is crucial in crafting messages that resonate with diverse audiences. By appreciating the intricacies of each language, linguists can adapt their communication style to suit the cultural expectations and preferences of their listeners.

Cultural sensitivity is key to successful multilingual communication. Each language carries with it a rich tapestry of traditions, customs, and social norms. A skilled linguist must navigate these cultural landscapes with grace, ensuring that their messages are not only understood but also respected. This requires a deep understanding of the cultural context in which the language is used, as well as an ability to empathize with the audience's perspective.

Non-verbal communication plays a significant role in conveying meaning across languages. Gestures, facial expressions, and body language can vary greatly between cultures, and what is considered polite in one culture may be perceived differently in another. A proficient linguist must be adept at reading and interpreting these non-verbal cues to enhance their verbal communication. This skill allows them to connect with their audience on a deeper level, fostering trust and rapport.

Finally, the power of language lies in its ability to inspire and influence. A linguist who can command multilingual audiences with grace and precision has the potential to bridge gaps, resolve conflicts, and create meaningful connections. By harnessing the power of language, linguists can become effective communicators, leaders, and advocates for cultural understanding and unity.

2

Chapter 2: The Art of Listening

Listening is an integral part of effective communication, especially when engaging with multilingual audiences. It is through active listening that a linguist can truly understand the needs, concerns, and preferences of their audience. This chapter delves into the art of listening, exploring techniques and strategies that linguists can employ to enhance their ability to connect with and engage their audience.

Active listening involves more than just hearing the words spoken; it requires paying attention to the speaker's tone, pitch, and pace, as well as their non-verbal cues. By doing so, a linguist can gain a deeper understanding of the speaker's emotions and intentions. This heightened awareness allows the linguist to respond more thoughtfully and empathetically, fostering a sense of trust and rapport.

One effective technique for active listening is paraphrasing. By restating the speaker's message in their own words, the linguist demonstrates that they have understood the key points and are genuinely interested in the conversation. This not only reinforces the speaker's message but also encourages further dialogue. Paraphrasing can be particularly useful when navigating complex or sensitive topics, as it provides an opportunity to clarify any misunderstandings and ensure that the conversation remains productive.

Another important aspect of active listening is asking open-ended questions. These questions encourage the speaker to elaborate on their thoughts and feelings, providing the linguist with more comprehensive insights into their perspective. Open-ended questions also signal to the speaker that their input is valued and respected, which can lead to more meaningful and engaging discussions.

In addition to verbal communication, non-verbal cues play a crucial role in active listening. Maintaining eye contact, nodding, and using appropriate facial expressions can convey attentiveness and interest. A linguist must also be mindful of their own body language, as it can either enhance or detract from the effectiveness of their communication. By cultivating positive non-verbal behaviors, the linguist can create a supportive and welcoming environment for their audience.

Finally, active listening involves being fully present in the moment. In today's fast-paced world, distractions are everywhere, making it challenging to focus entirely on the conversation at hand. However, a skilled linguist understands the importance of setting aside these distractions and dedicating their full attention to the speaker. This level of commitment not only improves the quality of the interaction but also strengthens the connection between the linguist and their audience.

3

Chapter 3: Crafting Clear Messages

The ability to convey messages clearly and effectively is a cornerstone of successful multilingual communication. This chapter focuses on the art of crafting clear and concise messages that resonate with diverse audiences. By employing strategies such as simplifying language, avoiding jargon, and using visual aids, linguists can ensure that their messages are understood and appreciated by all.

One of the primary challenges in multilingual communication is the potential for misunderstandings due to language differences. To mitigate this, linguists should strive to use simple and straightforward language. This means avoiding complex sentences and ambiguous phrases that may confuse the audience. By breaking down information into digestible chunks, the linguist can make their message more accessible to everyone, regardless of their language proficiency.

Jargon and technical terms can also be barriers to effective communication. While these terms may be familiar to the linguist, they may not be understood by the audience. To overcome this, linguists should either avoid using jargon altogether or provide clear explanations and definitions when necessary. This practice not only enhances comprehension but also demonstrates the linguist's commitment to making their message inclusive and accessible.

Visual aids are powerful tools that can complement verbal communication and enhance understanding. Diagrams, charts, and images can help illustrate complex concepts and provide context for the audience. When used effectively, visual aids can bridge language gaps and reinforce the key points of the message. Linguists should be mindful, however, of cultural differences in interpreting visual symbols and ensure that their visual aids are appropriate and meaningful for the audience.

Consistency is another important aspect of crafting clear messages. Linguists should maintain a consistent tone, style, and structure throughout their communication. This consistency helps establish a clear and coherent narrative, making it easier for the audience to follow and understand the message. Additionally, consistent use of terminology and phrasing can prevent confusion and reinforce key concepts.

Finally, feedback is a valuable tool for refining and improving communication. By actively seeking feedback from their audience, linguists can gain insights into how their messages are received and identify areas for improvement. This iterative process of feedback and refinement allows linguists to continuously enhance their communication skills and better serve their multilingual audiences.

4

Chapter 4: Building Rapport

Building rapport with an audience is essential for effective communication, especially in a multilingual context. Establishing a connection with the audience fosters trust, engagement, and a sense of mutual respect. This chapter explores techniques for building rapport, including finding common ground, showing empathy, and using humor appropriately.

Finding common ground is a fundamental step in building rapport. This involves identifying shared interests, values, or experiences that can serve as a foundation for the relationship. For linguists, this may include acknowledging the cultural heritage of the audience, discussing shared goals, or highlighting common challenges. By emphasizing these connections, the linguist can create a sense of unity and foster a positive, collaborative atmosphere.

Empathy is another critical component of building rapport. By putting themselves in the audience's shoes, linguists can better understand their needs, concerns, and emotions. This empathetic approach allows the linguist to tailor their messages to address the audience's specific context and demonstrate genuine care and consideration. Empathy also helps build trust, as the audience feels valued and understood.

Humor can be a powerful tool for building rapport, but it must be used carefully and appropriately. When used effectively, humor can lighten the mood, break down barriers, and create a sense of camaraderie. However, humor is highly culture-specific, and what may be funny in one culture could be offensive or misunderstood in another. Linguists should be mindful of these cultural differences and use humor in a way that is respectful and inclusive.

Active engagement with the audience is also crucial for building rapport. This involves encouraging participation, asking questions, and responding to the audience's input. By creating an interactive and dynamic environment, linguists can foster a sense of involvement and investment in the conversation. This engagement not only strengthens the connection between the linguist and the audience but also enhances the overall effectiveness of the communication.

Lastly, building rapport requires authenticity. Audiences are more likely to connect with and trust a linguist who is genuine and sincere. This means being honest about one's intentions, acknowledging any limitations, and showing a willingness to learn and adapt. Authenticity fosters a sense of credibility and reliability, which is essential for establishing a strong and lasting rapport with multilingual audiences.

5

Chapter 5: Adapting to Cultural Nuances

Understanding and respecting cultural nuances is vital for successful multilingual communication. Each culture has its own set of values, traditions, and communication styles that influence how messages are perceived and interpreted. This chapter delves into the importance of cultural awareness and provides strategies for adapting communication to suit different cultural contexts.

One of the key aspects of cultural awareness is recognizing that communication styles can vary widely between cultures. Some cultures may prioritize direct and explicit communication, while others may rely on more indirect and subtle cues. Linguists must be attuned to these differences and adapt their communication style accordingly. By doing so, they can ensure that their messages are both respectful and effective.

Understanding cultural norms and customs is also crucial for effective communication. This includes being aware of appropriate greetings, gestures, and forms of address, as well as understanding the cultural significance of certain symbols and practices. Linguists should take the time to research and learn about the cultural context of their audience to avoid misunderstandings and demonstrate respect for their traditions.

Language itself can reflect cultural values and priorities. For example, some languages may have specific words or expressions that convey concepts unique to that culture. Linguists should be mindful of these linguistic nuances and seek to understand their underlying cultural significance. This deeper understanding can enhance the linguist's ability to communicate in a way that resonates with the audience.

Flexibility is an essential trait for linguists working in multicultural environments. This means being open to adjusting one's communication style and approach based on the audience's cultural context. Flexibility also involves being willing to learn from mistakes and continuously improve one's cultural competence. By embracing flexibility, linguists can navigate cultural differences with ease and build stronger connections with their audience.

Finally, fostering intercultural dialogue is a valuable strategy for promoting understanding and collaboration. This involves creating opportunities for open and respectful conversations about cultural differences and similarities. By encouraging dialogue, linguists can facilitate mutual learning and appreciation, ultimately strengthening the bonds between diverse communities.

6

Chapter 6: Language as a Tool for Diplomacy

In today's globalized world, effective diplomacy relies heavily on language skills and cultural understanding. Linguists play a crucial role in bridging gaps between nations and fostering peaceful relations. This chapter explores how language can be used as a tool for diplomacy, highlighting key strategies and techniques for successful international communication.

One of the primary functions of diplomacy is to build and maintain relationships between countries. Language is a vital component of this process, as it facilitates dialogue and negotiation. Linguists who are skilled in multiple languages can serve as intermediaries, helping to translate not only words but also cultural nuances and intentions. This ability to navigate complex linguistic and cultural landscapes is essential for effective diplomacy.

Diplomatic language often requires a balance of tact and clarity. Messages must be delivered with precision to avoid misunderstandings, while also being sensitive to the cultural and political context of the audience. Linguists must be adept at crafting diplomatic language that is respectful, considerate, and strategic. This involves choosing words carefully, avoiding inflammatory or ambiguous language, and being mindful of the tone and implications of their messages.

Cultural competence is equally important in diplomatic communication. Understanding the cultural values and norms of the audience can help linguists tailor their messages to be more persuasive and impactful. This requires a deep appreciation of the historical, social, and political factors that shape the audience's perspective. By demonstrating cultural respect and awareness, linguists can build trust and credibility, which are essential for successful diplomatic relations.

In addition to verbal communication, non-verbal cues play a significant role in diplomacy. Gestures, body language, and facial expressions can convey respect, openness, and sincerity. Linguists must be skilled in interpreting and using non-verbal communication to reinforce their verbal messages and create a positive impression. This attention to detail can make a significant difference in diplomatic interactions.

Finally, language can be a powerful tool for conflict resolution and peacebuilding. By facilitating open and respectful dialogue, linguists can help address misunderstandings and find common ground. Language can also be used to promote empathy and understanding, fostering a sense of shared humanity. Through their linguistic skills, linguists have the potential to contribute to a more peaceful and interconnected world.

Chapter 7: Harnessing Technology for Multilingual Communication

Technology has revolutionized the way we communicate, providing new tools and platforms for multilingual interaction. This chapter explores how linguists can harness technology to enhance their communication skills and reach broader audiences. From translation software to social media, technology offers a wealth of opportunities for linguists to connect with people from diverse linguistic backgrounds.

Translation software has become increasingly sophisticated, making it easier for linguists to communicate across language barriers. While these tools are not a substitute for human expertise, they can be valuable aids in facilitating quick and efficient translation. Linguists can use translation software to complement their work, ensuring accuracy and consistency while saving time and effort. However, it is important for linguists to review and refine machine-generated translations to maintain the quality and cultural appropriateness of their messages.

Social media platforms offer unique opportunities for multilingual communication. Linguists can leverage these platforms to engage with audiences in real-time, sharing information, ideas, and perspectives. By creating content in multiple languages, linguists can reach a wider audience and foster cross-cultural dialogue. Social media also provides a space for interactive and dynamic communication, allowing linguists to respond to feedback and adapt their messages to the needs and preferences of their audience.

Webinars and virtual meetings have become essential tools for international communication. Linguists can use these platforms to conduct multilingual presentations, workshops, and discussions. The use of video, audio, and chat features enables linguists to convey their messages effectively and interact with participants from different linguistic backgrounds. Virtual meetings also offer the flexibility to connect with people across different time zones and geographical locations, making them ideal for global collaboration.

Language learning apps and online courses provide valuable resources for linguists to expand their language skills and cultural knowledge. These tools offer interactive and engaging learning experiences, allowing linguists to practice their language skills and gain insights into different cultures. By continuously improving their language proficiency, linguists can enhance their ability to communicate with diverse audiences and stay current with evolving linguistic trends.

Finally, artificial intelligence (AI) and machine learning technologies are transforming the field of linguistics. AI-powered language models can analyze and generate human-like text, providing valuable support for multilingual communication. Linguists can use these technologies to automate routine tasks, such as transcription and translation, and focus on more complex and creative aspects of their work. By embracing technology, linguists can stay at the forefront of multilingual communication and continue to make a positive impact in an increasingly interconnected world.

8

Chapter 8: The Role of Emotion in Communication

Emotions play a significant role in human communication, influencing how messages are perceived and interpreted. This chapter explores the importance of emotional intelligence in multilingual communication and provides strategies for effectively conveying and responding to emotions. By understanding and managing emotions, linguists can enhance their ability to connect with and engage their audience.

Emotional intelligence involves recognizing and understanding one's own emotions as well as those of others. For linguists, this means being attuned to the emotional undertones of their communication and being able to respond appropriately. This requires a high level of self-awareness and empathy, as well as the ability to regulate one's emotions to maintain a positive and constructive interaction.

One of the key aspects of emotional communication is the use of tone. The tone of voice can convey a wide range of emotions, from enthusiasm and excitement to frustration and anger. Linguists must be mindful of their tone and ensure that it aligns with the intended message. This is particularly important in multilingual communication, where tone can vary significantly between languages and cultures. By modulating their tone, linguists can convey their emotions effectively and create a more engaging and relatable communication experience.

Non-verbal cues also play a crucial role in emotional communication. Facial expressions, gestures, and body language can convey emotions more powerfully than words alone. Linguists must be skilled in interpreting and using non-verbal communication to enhance their verbal messages. This involves being aware of cultural differences in non-verbal cues and adapting one's behavior to suit the audience's expectations. By mastering non-verbal communication, linguists can create a more holistic and impactful communication experience.

Active listening is another essential component of emotional communication. By paying attention to the speaker's emotions and responding empathetically, linguists can build trust and rapport with their audience. This involves validating the speaker's feelings, showing genuine interest, and providing supportive feedback. Active listening not only enhances the emotional connection but also helps linguists to better understand the audience's needs and preferences.

Finally, managing emotions is critical for maintaining a positive and productive communication environment. Linguists must be able to regulate their emotions and respond calmly and professionally, even in challenging situations. This requires developing strategies for coping with stress, such as taking deep breaths, pausing to reflect, and seeking support from colleagues or mentors. By managing their emotions effectively, linguists can create a more harmonious and respectful interaction, fostering a sense of mutual understanding and collaboration.

9

Chapter 9: Public Speaking Across Languages

Public speaking is a skill that requires confidence, clarity, and adaptability, especially when addressing multilingual audiences. This chapter explores the techniques and strategies linguists can use to deliver effective speeches and presentations in multiple languages. By mastering the art of public speaking, linguists can captivate and inspire diverse audiences.

Preparation is key to successful public speaking. Linguists should thoroughly research their topic and audience, ensuring that they understand the cultural and linguistic context. This preparation allows linguists to tailor their message to the audience's needs and preferences, making it more relevant and engaging. Additionally, linguists should practice their speech in each language they plan to use, focusing on pronunciation, intonation, and pacing.

Clarity is essential in multilingual public speaking. Linguists should aim to deliver their message in a clear and concise manner, avoiding complex sentences and ambiguous phrases. Using simple and straightforward language ensures that the audience can easily follow and understand the speech. Linguists should also be mindful of their enunciation, speaking slowly and clearly to accommodate listeners who may not be fluent in the language.

Visual aids can enhance public speaking by providing additional context and reinforcing key points. Slides, diagrams, and images can help illustrate complex concepts and make the speech more engaging. Linguists should ensure that their visual aids are culturally appropriate and accessible to all audience members. By integrating visual elements, linguists can create a more dynamic and memorable presentation.

Engaging the audience is crucial for effective public speaking. Linguists can use techniques such as storytelling, anecdotes, and rhetorical questions to capture the audience's attention and make their message more relatable. Additionally, linguists should encourage audience participation, inviting questions and feedback to create an interactive and inclusive environment. This engagement not only enhances the audience's experience but also strengthens the connection between the speaker and the listeners.

Finally, confidence is a key factor in successful public speaking. Linguists should project confidence through their body language, eye contact, and vocal delivery. This confidence reassures the audience and reinforces the speaker's credibility. Linguists can build their confidence through practice, preparation, and positive self-talk. By believing in their ability to communicate effectively, linguists can deliver impactful and inspiring speeches that resonate with multilingual audiences.

10

Chapter 10: The Ethics of Multilingual Communication

Ethics play a critical role in multilingual communication, guiding linguists in their interactions with diverse audiences. This chapter examines the ethical considerations that linguists must navigate, including issues of accuracy, transparency, and cultural sensitivity. By adhering to ethical principles, linguists can ensure that their communication is respectful, honest, and responsible.

Accuracy is a fundamental ethical concern in multilingual communication. Linguists must strive to convey information accurately and avoid misrepresentations or distortions. This requires a commitment to thorough research and fact-checking, as well as a willingness to correct any errors or misunderstandings. By prioritizing accuracy, linguists can build trust and credibility with their audience.

Transparency is another important ethical principle. Linguists should be open about their intentions, sources, and potential biases. This transparency fosters accountability and allows the audience to make informed judgments about the information presented. Linguists should also disclose any conflicts of interest or affiliations that may influence their communication. By being transparent, linguists can promote ethical and responsible communication.

Cultural sensitivity is crucial for ethical multilingual communication.

Linguists must respect the cultural values, norms, and traditions of their audience, avoiding any language or behavior that could be perceived as disrespectful or offensive. This requires a deep understanding of the cultural context and a commitment to continuous learning and adaptation. By demonstrating cultural sensitivity, linguists can create a more inclusive and respectful communication environment.

Consent is an important consideration in multilingual communication. Linguists should seek permission before sharing personal stories, images, or information that involve others. This respect for privacy and autonomy helps protect the rights and dignity of individuals. Additionally, linguists should be mindful of the power dynamics in their interactions and strive to create an equitable and respectful dialogue.

Finally, ethical multilingual communication involves a commitment to promoting social justice and equality. Linguists can use their skills to amplify marginalized voices, challenge stereotypes, and advocate for positive change. By leveraging their linguistic expertise for the greater good, linguists can contribute to a more just and inclusive world.

11

Chapter 11: Overcoming Language Barriers

anguage barriers can pose significant challenges in communication, but linguists have the tools and strategies to overcome them. This chapter explores practical approaches to bridging language gaps and ensuring effective communication across linguistic boundaries. By addressing language barriers, linguists can create more inclusive and accessible interactions.

One effective strategy for overcoming language barriers is the use of interpreters and translators. Professional interpreters can facilitate real-time communication between speakers of different languages, ensuring that messages are accurately conveyed. Translators can provide written translations of documents, presentations, and other materials, making them accessible to a wider audience. Linguists should work closely with interpreters and translators to ensure that their messages are clear, accurate, and culturally appropriate.

Simplifying language is another valuable approach to addressing language barriers. Linguists should use plain language and avoid jargon, technical terms, and idiomatic expressions that may be difficult for non-native speakers to understand. By using clear and straightforward language, linguists can enhance comprehension and reduce the risk of misunderstandings.

Visual aids can also help bridge language gaps by providing additional context and support for verbal communication. Diagrams, charts, and images can illustrate key concepts and make information more accessible. Linguists should ensure that their visual aids are culturally relevant and appropriate, taking into account the audience's language and cultural background.

Technology offers a range of tools for overcoming language barriers. Translation apps, speech recognition software, and multilingual communication platforms can facilitate real-time translation and interpretation. Linguists can leverage these tools to enhance their communication and reach a broader audience. However, it is important to use technology judiciously and ensure that human expertise remains central to the communication process.

Cultural competence is essential for addressing language barriers. Linguists should invest time in learning about the cultural context of their audience, including social norms, values, and communication styles. This cultural awareness can help linguists tailor their messages to resonate with the audience and navigate potential challenges. By demonstrating cultural competence, linguists can create more meaningful and effective interactions.

12

Chapter 12: The Future of Multilingual Communication

The future of multilingual communication is shaped by technological advancements, evolving cultural dynamics, and the increasing interconnectedness of our world. This final chapter explores emerging trends and opportunities for linguists in the field of multilingual communication. By staying attuned to these developments, linguists can continue to innovate and make a positive impact.

Artificial intelligence (AI) and machine learning are transforming the landscape of multilingual communication. AI-powered language models can analyze, generate, and translate text with remarkable accuracy and speed. These technologies offer new possibilities for real-time translation, multilingual content creation, and personalized communication. Linguists can harness the power of AI to enhance their work, while also ensuring that ethical considerations and human expertise remain central to the communication process.

The rise of digital platforms and social media has created new opportunities for multilingual engagement. Linguists can use these platforms to connect with diverse audiences, share information, and foster cross-cultural dialogue. By creating content in multiple languages and leveraging interactive features, linguists can reach a global audience and promote cultural understanding.

Globalization and migration continue to shape the linguistic landscape, leading to the emergence of new language varieties and multilingual communities. Linguists must adapt to these changes by continuously expanding their language skills and cultural knowledge. This includes learning about hybrid languages, dialects, and linguistic innovations that reflect the dynamic nature of human communication.

Education and training play a crucial role in the future of multilingual communication. Linguists should invest in ongoing professional development, seeking out opportunities to learn new languages, refine their skills, and stay current with emerging trends. Educational institutions and organizations can support this growth by offering language courses, workshops, and resources that promote linguistic and cultural competence.

Finally, the future of multilingual communication is guided by a commitment to inclusivity and social justice. Linguists have the opportunity to use their skills to advocate for marginalized communities, challenge linguistic discrimination, and promote equitable access to information and opportunities. By embracing this mission, linguists can contribute to a more just and connected world.

Book Description

In **"The Linguist's Stage: Commanding Multilingual Audiences with Grace and Precision,"** embark on a journey that unveils the intricate art of multilingual communication. This insightful book takes readers through twelve meticulously crafted chapters, each elaborating on the nuances and techniques essential for linguists to engage, inspire, and connect with diverse audiences.

Starting with the power of language, the book delves into the significance of cultural context and non-verbal communication, emphasizing the foundational elements that make multilingual interactions impactful. As you progress, discover the art of listening, where active listening techniques and empathy play pivotal roles in understanding and responding to audience needs.

The chapters on crafting clear messages and building rapport provide valuable strategies for simplifying language, using visual aids, and establishing meaningful connections with audiences. Learn to adapt to cultural nuances, harness the potential of technology, and navigate the ethical considerations that shape responsible communication.

Explore the role of emotion in communication, and uncover the secrets of public speaking across languages, ensuring that your speeches are both captivating and clear. Overcoming language barriers and embracing future trends in multilingual communication are also covered, preparing linguists to thrive in an ever-evolving global landscape.

With practical approaches, real-world examples, and a focus on cultural competence, **"The Linguist's Stage"** is an essential guide for linguists, communicators, and anyone passionate about bridging linguistic divides. Command your multilingual audiences with grace and precision, and make a lasting impact in a world where language connects us all.